THE COMPLEAT GOLFER

By the la' Harry
'This shall not go for Nothing

COCK OF THE GREEN.

Portrait of the original golfing maniac, Andrew McKellar, died c. 1813. He played at Bruntsfield near Edinburgh and became so obsessed that he neglected his business, played by day, and after dark by the light of a lantern, and made his wife bring his meals out to the course

Knickerbocker suit from an advertisement for golfing attire, 1875-1900

THE COMPLEAT GOLFER
An illustrated history of the Royal and Ancient Game

Ian T. Henderson & David I. Stirk

London
Victor Gollancz Ltd
1985

Copyright © Henderson & Stirk Ltd
1982, 1985.

First published October 1982 by
Victor Gollancz Ltd
14 Henrietta Street
London WC2E 8QJ

Second edition with additional
material first published 1985

Created for the publishers by
Lund Humphries Publishers Ltd,
London

Designed by Christine Charlton
Typeset in Plantin by
TNR Productions Ltd, London
Printed in Great Britain by
Lund Humphries, Bradford

*British Library Cataloguing in
Publication Data*
Henderson, Ian T.
    The Compleat Golfer.—Rev ed.
    1. Golf—History—Pictorial works
    I.Title   II. Stirk, David I.
    796.352′09   GV963

ISBN 0-575-03732-6

Illustrations reproduced in this book
are taken from *Golf in the Making* and
Royal Blackheath published by
Henderson & Stirk Ltd and from *Fifty
Years of American Golf* by H.B. Martin
(Dodd, Mead & Company, New York
1936) and *Early Golf* by Steven van
Hengel (1983)

Contents

A sketch taken from Lauthier's *Treatise*
(Paris, 1717)) showing jeu de mail
(pall mall) being played (see page 11)

Introduction

This book presents a predominantly pictorial history of the game of golf.

It is widely believed among golfers that the game originated in Scotland. In fact, as we now know, it was the Dutch who appear to have invented it, playing a game called *Spel meten Kolven* from 1296 until the beginning of the eighteenth century when, mysteriously, this early form of golf went out of fashion and another game called 'Het Kolven', a sort of mini-golf, often played indoors, took its place. Records exist of golf being played in forty Dutch townships, with edicts against playing the game in the streets. By the end of the sixteenth century, Dutch and Flemish artists were sketching and painting, in dozens of landscapes and on a wealth of tiles, a remarkable record of life in Holland; and there is abundant evidence from these illustrations that life in Holland at this period included the game of golf.

Everyone always assumes that the Normans under William I invaded and conquered Britain in 1066, and so they did, but few know that the right wing of his army was made up of Flemings under the command of the Duc de Boulogne. Some of his Flemish followers were ultimately rewarded with extensive lands in Scotland. From that developed, over the centuries, the close ties between Scotland and the Low Countries – a major part of the Scottish aristocracy is of Flemish descent. The Scottish Royal Family had Flemish blood in them, and Holland and Scotland today share the same national emblem – the Lion Rampant.

From 1297 until around 1700 the Dutch played a national game which we can only call golf, leaving a pictorial record which is unique in the annals of any sport. However, they gave it up around 1700. In 1457 a Scots Act of Parliament mentions golf for the first time and thereafter there are frequent printed references to golf until the first pictorial evidence of the game appears in 1746. Happily for the future of the game, Scottish Freemasons took over where the Dutch left off. They formed the first organised societies in the mid-eighteenth century who played golf as a healthy form of exercise prior to wining and dining.

The great development of the game can be attributed to the wonderful strides made in perfecting the ball; and the arrival of the rubber golf ball in 1848 made the game considerably cheaper and therefore available to more people. Prior to that date, when the feathery ball was in use, golf clubs had long, wooden heads; a single iron club might be in the player's bag for use in really difficult situations but the main reason why iron clubs were not used more often was because the feathery ball could easily be burst by an iron club and at that time balls were as expensive as clubs. With the arrival of the rubber ball iron clubs were used increasingly and before long there were more iron clubs than wooden ones in the golf bag; and there were many more golfers. Nevertheless, golf did not become a national game in Scotland until the 1890s when it spread all over the world, particularly to the USA. To the Scots, therefore, must be given the credit for keeping the game alive for so many years and preserving it for posterity. It was they who were to make it so popular throughout the world, and thousands of Scotsmen left their shores to establish and teach the game in the farthest corners of the earth.

Those readers who wish to pursue the history of golf in greater detail are referred to three other books. Two are by the authors, Ian T. Henderson and David I. Stirk: *Golf in the Making* (1979) which contains all that is known about early club- and ball-makers, the clubs themselves, patents, etc., and *Royal Blackheath* (1981) which explains how groups of Freemasons were responsible for the formation of the first Golfing Societies and how the Royal Blackheath Golf Club itself helped to spread the game throughout England and other parts of the world. The third is *Early Golf* by Steven van Hengel (1983) which relates the full documented story of Dutch golf from its inception and is a really splendid piece of research.

Match at Blackheath, by F. Gilbert,
1869

The Origins of Golf

That golf is an ancient game is undeniable but its origins and its relationship with other games which involved striking a ball with some form of club have so far not been resolved. The Romans played a game called 'Paganica' using a leather ball stuffed with flock and in England in the fourteenth century a similar game called 'cambuca' was played with a wooden ball, but we do not know what kind of club was used to hit the ball in either case.

The sketch of the stained-glass roundel from the Battle of Crecy window in Gloucester Cathedral, c. 1350, and the Araucanian Indian boy from Chile, taken from *The Zoology of the Voyage of HMS Beagle* which describes Charles Darwin's famous voyage c. 1835 are illustrations whose resemblance must be accepted as a coincidence. There is no clue as to what form of game is being played, and all that can be deduced is that from early times in various parts of the world striking a ball with a stick was a form of activity that attracted adherents — call it what you will

Pall mall, or jeu de mail, the stroke for which, from all descriptions, closely resembled the golf swing as shown on page 6. The game originated in Italy, was taken up by the French and came to England early in the seventeenth century. The original course in London was Pall Mall, St James's. This was later moved to The Mall, and both names recall their original use to this day. The pair of clubs and a wooden ball taken from a house at No. 68 Pall Mall still survive in the British Museum. It is hard to see how this game, from which croquet originated, could have influenced the development of golf

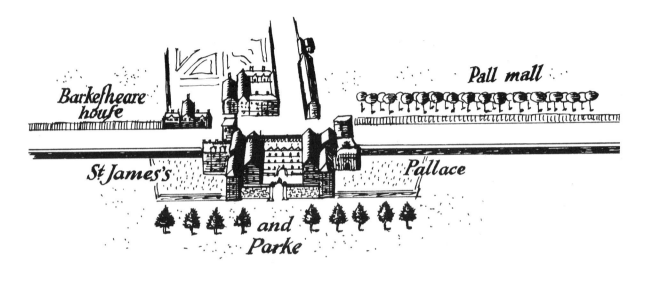

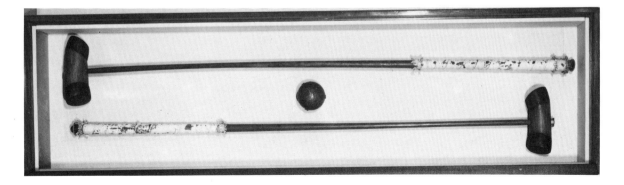

Dutch Golf

The beginnings of golf have been traced to the village of Loenen in 1296 and there are documentary records of the game being played in no less than forty places in Holland. There were frequent edicts banning play in the streets and city authorities were forever attempting to confine players to areas outside the city on the ramparts. In the winter the game was played on the ice. The 'Long Game' then played was called 'Spel meten Kolven'.

Pictures from the sixteenth and seventeenth centuries provide an illustrated golfing record unique in the annals of any sport. The marvellous Dutch landscape paintings of these years show that people in Holland were playing a form of golf, with enthusiasm, up to the early eighteenth century, when the game inexplicably died out. In many a crowded scene, on ice or land, tiny figures may be observed, club in hand. There are numerous portraits of children holding a club rather than a toy, and, in all, there are nearly 500 illustrations, together with a fascinating number of Dutch tiles, all of which relate to the game.

So far no contemporary description of the game or its rules has been found but there is evidence of a hole being used, and on ice a pole, often decorated, was adopted instead.

We show on page 16 early seventeenth-century metal club heads and a wooden ball, with a modern ball for comparison, all found in excavations in Amsterdam. No example of a seventeenth-century wooden club has so far been found. Leather balls, stuffed with horsehair, flock or feathers were in general use and their mode of construction can be observed in many of the portraits. Similar types of balls were also produced in large numbers for hand tennis (*Kaatsen*), an ancient game which is still played today. The ball manufacturers did a large export business throughout the Continent and also shipped balls to Scotland (and there is evidence that Scotland, in turn, shipped wooden clubs to Holland in the mid-seventeenth century). The ball-making craft survives to this day.

When the game died out and all evidence of play disappeared, its place was taken by *Kolf*, or *Het kolven*, a short distance (and often indoor) game, which might be termed mini-golf, using heavier rigid clubs and large balls. This game in turn was to lose its popularity, although still played when the Scottish version of the game arrived at The Hague in 1890.

One of the two maps on page 17 indicates the places where golf is known to have been played prior to 1700. It is clear from this and from contemporary pictures that the Dutch game of golf was a national game. The other map shows the places in Scotland where golf is believed to have been played, circa 1650. These coastal regions were places where trade with Holland was likely to have been carried on. It is not without significance that golf did not spread to the west of Scotland until the middle of the nineteenth century. Whereas golf in Holland was a national game, it never became really popular in Scotland on account of the considerable expense of playing, until the great golf craze at the end of the nineteenth century.

The Dutch in the USA
It is recorded that in March 1657, in Fort Orange (now Albany), New York, a charge was laid before the magistrates of playing golf in the streets and causing damage. This was followed in 1659 by an ordinance prohibiting all playing of golf in the streets. There is evidence that between 1793 and 1799, a 'Kolf Baan Club' was in existence at Charleston.

The recent recovery from a Dutch East Indiaman wrecked off the Shetland Isles in 1656, when on its way to Batavia, of five club heads confirms that the Dutch were taking their national game overseas. That golf was being played at Fort Orange in 1657 was not unusual and the Dutch may have been playing golf in those other parts of North America which they colonised.

A player with the ball teed up in the snow

Sketch after a Flemish Book of Hours, 1501

Sketches of golfers extracted from
seventeenth-century Dutch landscapes

Early seventeenth-century club
fragments and wooden ball with
modern ball for comparison

Wooden ball, *c.* 1590

Leather-covered ball enlarged from
sketch below (*c.* 1612)

Taken from a painting by an unknown
Flemish artist, and reputed to be the
eldest son of James I in 1595

Golf in progress, supported by the
necessary refreshment. After Hendrick
Avercamp

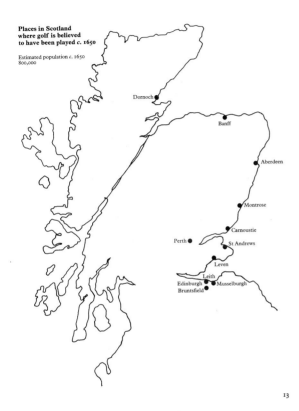

Places in Scotland where golf is
believed to have been played *c.* 1650

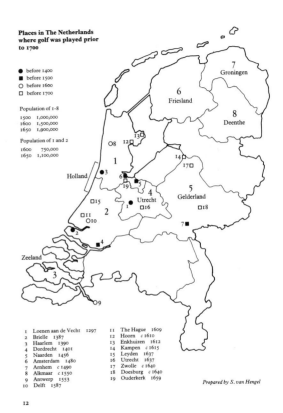

1	Loenen aan de Vecht	1297	11	The Hague	1609
2	Brielle	1387	12	Hoorn	*c* 1610
3	Haarlem	1390	13	Enkhuizen	1612
4	Dordrecht	1401	14	Kampen	*c* 1615
5	Naarden	1456	15	Leyden	1637
6	Amsterdam	1480	16	Utrecht	1637
7	Arnhem	*c* 1490	17	Zwolle	*c* 1640
8	Alkmaar	*c* 1550	18	Doesburg	*c* 1640
9	Antwerp	1553	19	Ouderkerk	1659
10	Delft	1587			

Prepared by S. van Hengel

Places in the Netherlands where golf
was played prior to 1700

Early Golf

Bruntsfield, Edinburgh, with a view of the Castle in the background and the Golfers' Inn, which still stands today, in the foreground. A watercolour painted by Paul Sandby RA in 1746 (courtesy of the Trustees of the British Museum). The site of the course still exists but the view of the Castle is obstructed. Visitors may still pitch and putt there with replicas of the old long-headed wooden clubs

William St Clair of Roslin. Grand Master Mason of Scotland: he laid the foundation stone of the Golf House at Leith in 1767 for the Company of Edinburgh Golfers, assisted by fourteen 'worthy members of the golfing company', all Masons

Above left: Portrait of Old Alick, the
hole-maker at Royal Blackheath

Left: the oldest surviving hole-cutter,
dated 1829, Royal Musselburgh

Above: 'Stymied', from a Dublin print

Before the days of a regulation hole and teeing ground, the ball was teed up with sand taken from the bottom of the hole, either one or two club-lengths from it. This photograph was taken at Edinburgh, *c.* 1860

Left: Edward, Prince of Wales at Oxford in 1912, about to bicycle off to play golf

MR. WILLIAM THOMSON.   ADMIRAL MAITLAND DOUGALL.   SANDY PIRIE.   Colonel J. FAIRLIE.   TOM MORRIS.
MR. GEORGE WHYTE MELVILLE.   MR. GEORGE GLENNIE.   MR. GILMOUR.
PLAYERS AT ST. ANDREWS IN THE 'SIXTIES'

The picture above shows a group of professionals at St Andrews in the 1860s

A *Punch* cartoon of the 1890s with the caption 'The Golf Stream' — a comment on the golf craze of the time

'Holed Out' — Louis Wain, the Victorian artist who drew cats as humans, catches the spirit of the age

The first golfing society in England was established on the Heath at Blackheath, London. Above: The Green Man public house, for many years the headquarters of the Royal Blackheath Club, now demolished

Medal day at Royal Blackheath, 1875

The Gold Medal shown here is the oldest in the history of the game and dates from 1792 when it was made for the Knuckle Club, a Masonic organisation subsequently disbanded, 'the members in future merely to meet as golfers'

Another example of an early gold medal from Loretto House Golf Club, Musselburgh, 1854

Professionals playing at Royal
Blackheath, 1890

Sketch taken from the centre design of
the Knuckle Club Medal

Eighteenth-century golf in the Southern States of America

A nineteenth-century walnut ballot box, formerly the property of the Honourable Company of Edinburgh Golfers. The voting for membership was done using small wooden balls, each voter having one ball. The candidate's visiting card was placed in the spear-shaped holder on the top of the box, so that all knew for whom they were voting. The ball was placed in the Yes or No drawer to register the vote by putting the hand containing the ball into the trumpet-shaped orifice; the ball could then be dropped into either drawer without disclosing the vote to an onlooker. After the voting was complete, the two drawers were unlocked and the votes counted.
Courtesy of Phillips in Chester

Before looking at all the evidence of golfing activity, it is essential, as in the case of Holland, to look at the state of the game in Scotland and at the Scottish outpost at Blackheath, whose history must first be examined. This is the history of the first Golf Club ever to be established outside Scotland, and the arrival of golf in England is attributed to James VI of Scotland becoming James I of England and bringing a large Scottish Court with him to London in 1604. Thus golf arrived at Blackheath as the result of a predominantly Scottish Court being in residence at Greenwich Palace, on the Thames near London.

An examination of the Blackheath records, however, revealed an entirely new explanation as to how organised golf was started both in Scotland and at Blackheath. The feature of all early Golfing Societies was their commitment to dining and conviviality. This can be understood now that we know that it was groups of Freemasons who had the happy idea of adding golf as a healthy form of exercise prior to their dining. They had Club uniforms, ceremonies, fines in the form of drink for absence or other offences; toasts, including the Masonic 'three times three'. New membership was controlled with the use of the ballot box. Attendance at dinners and guests were recorded, as were often the details of the meals. There was never a great deal in those days to mention about golf, except the bets on the matches, which were usually entered in a separate book, and were by no means all related to golf matches.

The fact that these societies were organised on similar lines could have been no accident, and once the Grand Master Mason of Scotland, Sinclair of Roslin, and his fellow Freemasons had been observed laying the foundation stone of a new golfing house at Leith in 1767 there can hardly be any doubt that the attractive concept of playing golf before banqueting was organised by them. Golf historians up to now have never been able to explain why there was the obligation to dine after playing golf; nor have they looked at the activities of the early Scots as a whole. We believe that the explanations now offered permit the history of these early societies to be examined on a far more logical basis.

'This day William St. Clair of Roslin Esquire, the
Undoubted representative of the honourable and heritable
G.M.M. of SCOTLAND In the presence of Alexander Keith
Esquire Captain of the honourable Company of Golfers and

other worthy members of the Golfing Company, all Masons, the G: (sic) now in his GRAND CLIMAX of Golfing laid the foundation stone of the Golfing House in the S.E. Corner thereof by THREE STROKES with the MALLETT

Alexr Peacocke M.M.   Alexr Keith Capt.
Wm. ST: Clair G.M.M.
Robert Henderson
Alexr Duncan M.M.
   Capt Blackheath &
   Old Capt. of St Andrews
James Cheape
William Hogart
Alexr Orme M.M.
Robert Beatson M.M.
Henry Bethune G.M.
Richard Tod Sub. G.M.
Henry Seton 2 Capt. M.M.
Ben Gordon'

The definition of the Masonic Fraternity is given as: 'An oathbound fraternal order of men derived from the mediaeval fraternity of stonemasons in England and Europe'.

Readers interested in the development of Freemasonry in the United States are referred to the *Encyclopaedia Americana*. In 1977 there were 4 million Freemasons in the USA, organised in 49 Grand Lodges and 15,770 lodges. Thirteen presidents, including George Washington, have been Freemasons. The first recorded lodge was in Boston in 1733.
It is fortunate that the Freemasons became interested in golf as a healthy form of exercise prior to their fraternal and convivial dinners in the mid and late eighteenth century, as, without their organising ability, we might not today be playing that delightful, but exasperating, game that we know as golf.

Freemasons shared a secret, and as time went on, they played golf with non-Masons, who were not admitted to their ceremonies, or mysteries, as they were referred to. It will have been noticed that the Burgess, Bruntsfield, Musselburgh and Blackheath Societies all have foundation dates earlier than their first Minutes, and that considerable parts of the Edinburgh Company's Minutes are missing. We believe that the explanation for these missing minutes lies in the admission of non-Masons to the Societies, owing to the decline in the number of Masons who were golfers. Once this process reached a certain stage, the Societies decided to destroy any evidence which might reveal their secrets. By this means they were remarkably successful in covering their tracks for so many years, and this was done in accordance with masonic practice. Nevertheless, some of the original Societies have been left with a strong sense of tradition, the origins of which present members are unlikely to be aware of. This explains why the majority of the original Societies still have no lady membership. All that we can say with certainty is that these early Societies had similar customs not related to golf; they shared a secret – again not related to golf – and they were not formed with the primary object of playing golf. What was originally offered was, in today's terminology, a 'package deal' – golf, dinner and the mysteries.

At all events, they succeeded in keeping the game alive, when it might so easily have suffered the same fate as golf in Holland, and disappeared. Dining and conviviality belonged to that age, and golf was a most useful associate: simple and straightforward to play, 'the very healthy exercise of the golf', as it was called.

The arrival of golf in America

Our research into the Port of Leith (near Edinburgh) records disclosed a large shipment of 96 clubs and 432 balls to Charleston, South Carolina in 1743. This was at a time when the first Societies or Clubs were being formed in Scotland. In due course, the South Carolina Golf Club was formed in 1786, followed by the Savannah Golf Club in 1795. To the shipments already mentioned must be added the following further information which has recently come to light:

Extract from Customer Accounts Book, Port of Leith
10.5.1743 in [the ship] *Magdalen* William Course for David Deas, South Carolina (Charlston): 8 doz golf clubs, 3 gross golf balls.

Extract from Greenock (Glasgow) Customs Accounts
23.10.1750 in the *William Irvine*, John McLean, Master, for Virginia – 1 doz golf clubs, 12 doz golf balls.
27.2.1751 for Virginia – 4 doz golf clubs, 2 groce golf balls.
23.4.1751 in the *Jean of Glasgow*, John Modervell, Master; for Virginia – 1 doz golf clubs and balls.
(In 1753 there was even a shipment to St Petersburgh in Russia).

Extract from Glasgow Customs Accounts
26th February 1765 a shipment to Maryland of 1½ doz golf clubs and 1 groce golf balls.

Thus in the period 1743–65, 186 clubs and almost 1000 balls were shipped, and substantial shipments must have supported the subsequent founding of the Charleston and Savannah Clubs.

To the quite considerable amount of further information which has appeared in the last few years, must be added facts in the publication *The Carolina Low Country – Birthplace of American Golf, 1786* by Charles Price and George C. Rogers Jr (Sea Pines Company, Hilton Head Island, USA, 1980).

The first golf shipment of all to Carolina in 1743 was to David Deas, who was in partnership with his brother John as merchants certainly by 1748; and according to Colonel Alston Deas, a direct descendant, the family tradition has always maintained that the family introduced golf to America and, furthermore, that John Deas, a member of the Kilwinnig Lodge of Charleston, was the first Provincial Grand Master in America. (The Grand Lodge of Charleston was formed in 1772.) John Deas died in 1790. The golf tradition is now supported by fact, and the Masonic tradition is hardly surprising, but needs verifying by a Masonic historian. It is understood that the Charleston Grand Lodge records are now held in Columbia.

John and David Deas' father was a ship-owner in Leith and his sons must have learned golf on Leith Links – a five-hole course shown on the map overleaf – and that would probably have been their model when they set up a course in Charleston. Blackheath, London also started with five holes around the same time; two of them were named after Leith – Thorntree and Braehead. Even the original links at St Andrews had only nine holes.

The first shipment of clubs and balls took place in 1743, one year prior to the public appearance of the Hon. Company of Edinburgh Golfers in 1744 (and the first ever Rules of Golf and the competition for the Silver Putter), whose members had already formed the habit of dining together as Freemasons after playing golf as a healthy exercise. This was the enjoyable package deal that the Deas brothers must have been intent upon introducing to their fellow Scotsmen in Charleston.

Once these facts are appreciated all that is at present known regarding golf on the Eastern seaboard of the USA can be understood. Golf must have been played by small groups of Scottish Masons up and down the coast, until finally Charleston and Georgia were sufficiently established to become public Clubs, having played together long before the so-called foundation dates of 1786 and 1795. Thereafter they commemorated these dates annually (by notices in the press) in exactly the same way as Societies did in Britain. (Royal Blackheath have been doing it without a break, except for war years, since 1789.)

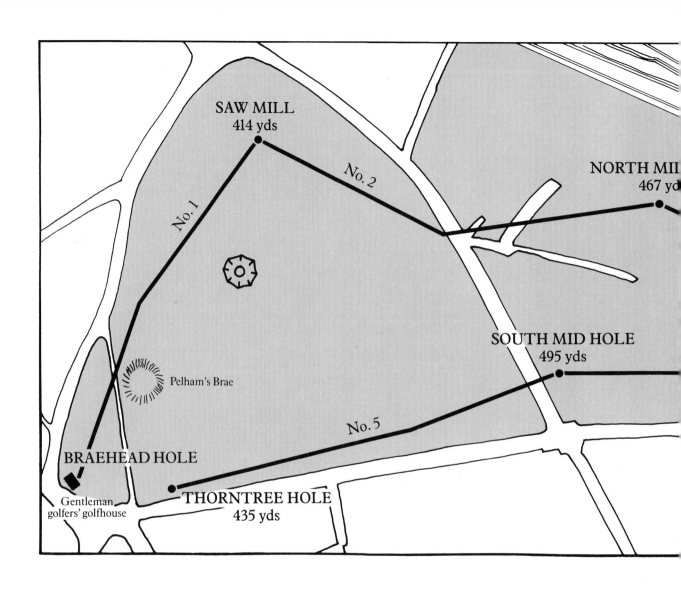

SAW MILL
414 yds

No. 2

No. 1

NORTH MIL
467 yd

SOUTH MID HOLE
495 yds

Pelham's Brae

No. 5

BRAEHEAD HOLE

Gentleman
golfers' golfhouse

THORNTREE HOLE
435 yds

Taken from a map prepared by
Lieut-Colonel Bryan Evans Lombe.

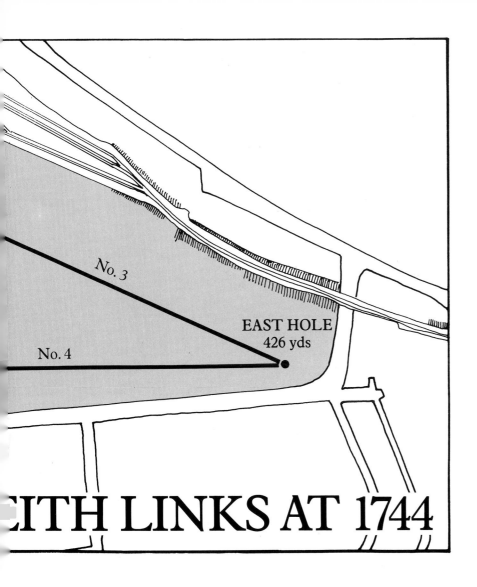

No. 3

No. 4

EAST HOLE
426 yds

:ITH LINKS AT 1744

South Carolina Golf Club

James Gairdner, President; William Blacklock, Vice-President; William Milligan, Secretary and Treasurer. This society dine together once a fortnight at their Club-House on Harleston's Green; the day of meeting is Saturday.
– May, 1796

The Anniversary of the South-Carolina Golf Club will be held on Saturday the 21st instant, at the Club House on Harleston's Green, where the members are requested to attend at one o'clock.

William Milligan, Secretary

Charleston City Gazette, 12 October 1797

There remains the question, which has concerned golf historians – why no details whatever of golf? First, they do not appear to have put up any trophies for competition by medal play such as the home Societies had done (in those days medal play was never really popular – match play was always preferred.) Golf journalism was unheard of, so even mentions of golfing activities were few and far between; nor is it surprising that no documented clubs or balls have survived, for very few eighteenth-century clubs or balls have survived anywhere, but for a unique example see page 68.

Finally, any evidence of the game being played in the USA peters out in 1812 – at a time when the game was in the doldrums in Britain – only the arrival of the gutta percha golf ball in 1848 revived its popularity. The Dutch gave up their long game (Spel meten Kolven) after 1700, and the Southern States of America gave up their game sometime after 1812 and did not take it up again until the 1880s by which time it had become a vastly more interesting game.

St Andrews Yonkers, New York – 1888 and thereafter
Golf was established in Montreal, Canada in 1873, but it was not until the late 1880s that there were numerous attempts to popularise the game in the USA. The survivor and now the acknowledged first Club of the new golf era was St Andrews Yonkers Club in 1888.

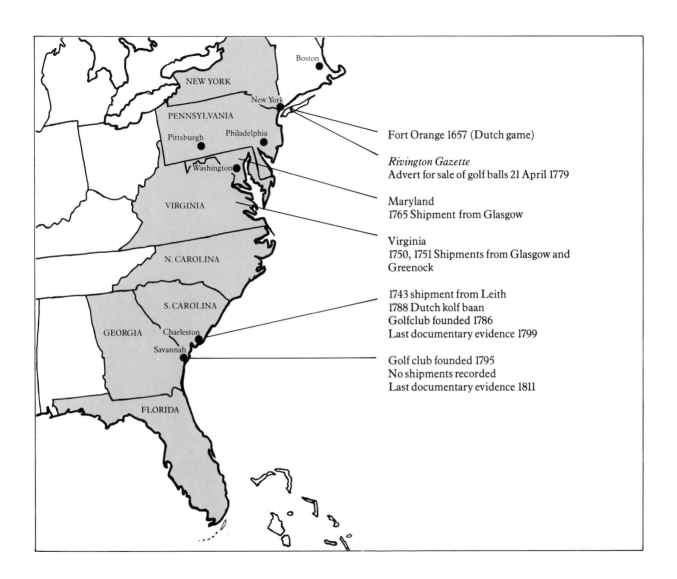

Fort Orange 1657 (Dutch game)

Rivington Gazette
Advert for sale of golf balls 21 April 1779

Maryland
1765 Shipment from Glasgow

Virginia
1750, 1751 Shipments from Glasgow and
Greenock

1743 shipment from Leith
1788 Dutch kolf baan
Golfclub founded 1786
Last documentary evidence 1799

Golf club founded 1795
No shipments recorded
Last documentary evidence 1811

Thereafter, in the 25 years up to World War I, the game expanded in the most remarkable way and after the War the United States not only had produced the leading players in the world but dominated the equipment market.

The game in America could never have been expanded so quickly if it had not attracted hundreds of young men from Britain to better themselves, and a knowledge of golf was often the only asset which they carried overseas.

As H.B. Martin (*Fifty Years of American Golf*, 1936) wrote, they came singly, they came in pairs and they came collectively – entire families embarking in one ship, such as the Smiths and Maidens, both from Carnoustie, whose pupils collected no less than twenty-eight national Championships.

The famous Smith family of golfers who came over from Carnoustie, Scotland in the 1890s.

The Haskell Ball and the Gammeter
ball-making machine.

In August 1898 G. Work and Coburn
Haskell registered the first golf-ball
patent in the USA and it was followed
in 1900 by one of the most important
developments in the history of golf –
J. R. Gammeter's patent for machine-
winding the elastic thread round the
core of the Haskell. This revolutionised
golf-ball manufacture – and turned
them out by the hundred. Haskell's
name is remembered today but it was
Gammeter who created the machine
that made the ball such an outstanding
success.

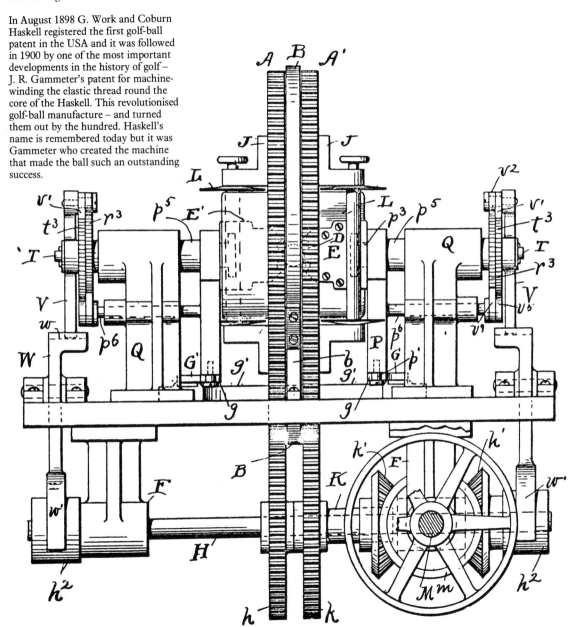

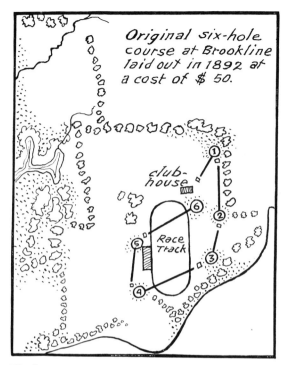

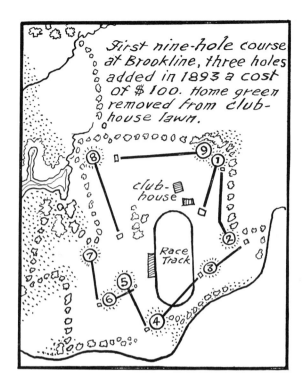

The first six-hole course, and the first nine-hole course at Brookline, Mass.

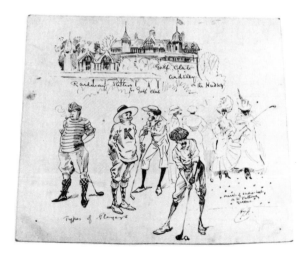

Pen cartoon by Henry Furniss of clubhouse and players at Ardsley on Hudson. Note the marks of ladies' heels on the putting green (bottom right).
Courtesy of Phillips in Chester

The Country Club in Brookline, in the late 1880s. Horse races were more important than golf in those days.

Golf at The Country Club was started as a result of it being demonstrated to a member by Miss Boit on a visit from Pau, France, who brought golf clubs with her, when visiting the Honeywell family in Boston.

The Country Club in the middle 1890s. Golf was beginning to become popular.

A scene on the Shinnecock Hills
course at Southampton (USA) in 1892.
This is the oldest incorporated Golf
Club in the United States and the first
to build a clubhouse, which was
designed by Stanford White.

Players in the first American Amateur
Championship, 1894. St Andrews
Yonkers, New York.

The first 'official' golf champions of the United States. Charles B. Macdonald (above) who won the amateur title and Horace Rawlins (above left) who won the open title at Newport in 1895.

Willie Dunn Jr. (1865-1952) was Professional Champion of America, 1894. He designed and constructed the course at Shinnecock Hills, Long Island, USA, c. 1890.

Charles B. Macdonald, the first official winner of the American amateur title, in 1895. His family originally came from St Andrews. He subsequently took a leading part in promoting the game, in forming the U.S. Golf Association and in maintaining its links with St Andrews, thus ensuring that the world still plays under the same rules

The famous caricature of Walter J.
Travis (above left) when he won the
British Open Amateur Championship
in 1904. Travis in 1909 (above right)
and (below) in the redcoat era in 1898.
See also page 98.

Some cartoons which appeared in
Punch around the turn of the century

THE AMERICAN HUSBAND

THE ENGLISH WIFE

In America the ladies, from the beginning, refused to accept a subordinate position in golf, unlike their British counterparts who, whether they liked it or not, were not welcomed as club members. Even today this situation exists in a few clubs

LINK(S)ED SWEETNESS

The Real Caddie (*audibly*). " This club is going to ruin — allowing all these ladies to join ! "
Miss Sharp. " They evidently can't get gentlemen ! "

The first Ladies' Golf Club at
Westward Ho!, was formed in 1868.
The Ladies had their own 9-hole
course, separate from the main course,
and their own professional, who was
only allowed to teach them. All is
decorum in this picture; it is clearly
more important not to show an ankle
than to have a good golf swing; nor did
the decorative dress suggest that a full
golf swing was possible. The clubhouse
is a tent, erected for the day

The Golf Ball

The great development of the game of golf can be directly attributed to progress made in perfecting the ball, making it a more pleasant game to play. The ball in use until the middle of the nineteenth century was what is known as a 'feathery'. This was a leather ball — not unlike a fives ball to look at — stuffed with wet feathers, which became very hard when it dried out. It flew when dry, but wheezed through the air in wet conditions and could easily be destroyed by an injudicious stroke with an iron club. At a price of up to 4s 0d each, the feathery ball was expensive, costing almost as much as a club. The most important development in the history of golf was the use of rubber in making a ball. 'Gutta percha', a hard substance which could be softened in hot water, was discovered in Malaya in 1843. In 1848 the first rubber golf-balls appeared, made very simply by immersing the 'gutta percha' in hot water and rolling it by hand into round balls, which hardened as they dried out. These smooth round balls, however, would not fly properly at first, but it was discovered that this defect could be rectified by indenting them with a hammer. They would not accept white paint and were dark yellow or brown in colour, but they were cheap and would last forever. This discovery immediately put the game within reach of those who could not afford the 'feathery'. By the 1880s the 'gutty' or hard composite ball began to appear —a ball so hard that it had a decisive effect on the design of wooden clubs. Club heads could shatter on impact. Sometimes even the balls themselves shattered.

Then out of the blue came the next great advance — the arrival in 1898 of the Haskell core-wound rubber ball, invented and developed in America. This at once made the game easier and more pleasant to play. The ball could fly yards further and even when mis-hit, the results were not so disastrous. This ball was relatively expensive, and cost 2s 6d, whereas iron clubs were 3s 6d and woods 5s 0d. But the improvement was so decisive that price did not matter. The innovation also affected every golf course, all of them in the end having to be lengthened to accommodate the new ball. It was not until 1922 that the size of the ball was first standardised (there are now two sizes). Before that any size of ball could be used. Today's ball is little recognised for the marvel of ingenuity that it is. A direct descendant of the Haskell, it is now at a price which, amazingly, is only a fraction of the price of a new club.

Golf balls prior to 1900

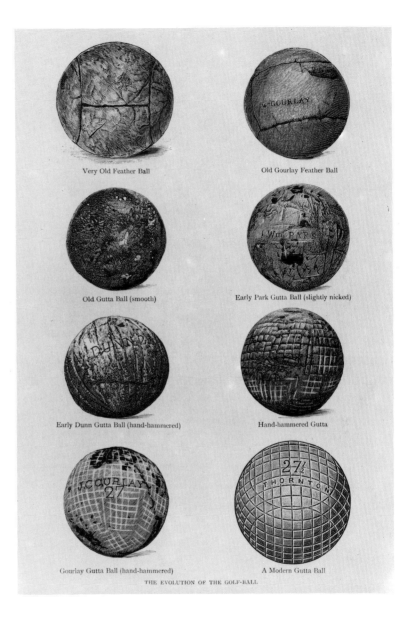

Very Old Feather Ball

Old Gourlay Feather Ball

Old Gutta Ball (smooth)

Early Park Gutta Ball (slightly nicked)

Early Dunn Gutta Ball (hand-hammered)

Hand-hammered Gutta

Gourlay Gutta Ball (hand-hammered)

A Modern Gutta Ball

THE EVOLUTION OF THE GOLF-BALL

Top (left to right): Dunlop Maxfli, c. 1922; Rubber-cored Springvale Hawk, c. 1907; Cestrian gutty, c. 1900. Above: home-made gutta, and sheet of gutta percha from which it was made

Golf-ball box

THE "ECLIPSE" GOLF BALL.
(CURRIE'S PATENT.)

THESE have quite superseded the old gutta-percha balls. They are almost indestructible, no club or iron will hack them, they fly beautifully, and retain their perfectly round shape; they can be driven further than the gutta-percha ball, and are quite true on the putting-green.

EXTRACT FROM "THE FIELD," 23RD JULY, 1881. —"We have thoroughly tested the specimens sent, and were agreeably surprised to find how near they came to the high estimate put upon them by the Patentee. Most assuredly they do not get hacked; not only did we play for four hours with the one ball, but for nearly two minutes afterwards we hammered away at it with our niblick, and no trace of hacking could be found. A better driving ball, too, we never struck; but the very elasticity which constituted its excellence in that particular at first rendered it somewhat uncertain in the short or putting game, especially where the green was a bit rough. That drawback, on our calling attention to it, the Patentee has remedied, and a fresh trial has convinced us that the remedy is effectual. As to the alterations effected by change of temperature, we cannot, in this tropical weather, speak from experience; but every Golfer knows that during intense frost the gutta-percha balls occasionally split, and these we are assured will not."

THE "ECLIPSE" GOLF BALL.—The "Eclipse" continues to grow in favour with golfers, as the unsolicited testimony of experts abundantly testifies. At the commencement of last season it for a time lost its good name; complaints as to chipping, splitting, and durability —or, rather, non-durability—were frequent, and, as the patentee speedily discovered, not without cause. The increased demand for the ball had necessitated the construction of new machinery, and in the augmented plant was found a flaw which accounted for the shortcoming. This, however, has since been remedied. A correspondent writes that he has played every alternate day for two months with a couple of these balls selected at random, and never drove any that gave such entire satisfaction.—*Field*, April 2nd, 1887.

Messrs. Currie, of the Caledonian Rubber Works, Edinburgh, are the patentees of the "Eclipse" Golf Ball, which, since they first introduced it, has been greatly improved in flying qualities. No less authority than Mr. Horace Hutchinson, the amateur champion, has pronounced the opinion that in its all round merit, the "Eclipse" is quite as good as the Gutta Ball. There can be no doubt about the "Eclipse" being the better ball to play with against the wind; it also retains its roundness, a great desideratum in putting, and is the most economical ball of the two.—The *Newcastle Daily Journal*, April 14th, 1887.

To be had from all Indiarubber Depots and Golf Club Makers.

PATENTEES AND SOLE MAKERS,

WILLIAM CURRIE & CO.,

Caledonian Rubber Works, Dalry Road, Edinburgh.

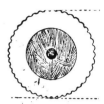

THE PLAIN SOLID GUTTA PERCHA BALL WITH SCRATCHED OR HAMMERED SURFACE. THIS DISPLACED THE FEATHER BALL.

THE GUTTA PERCHA BALL, WITH CUT LINE MARKING; POPULAR FOR A PERIOD.

THE GUTTA PERCHA BALL WITH BRAMBLE MARKING. THIS WAS THE LAST OF THE HOMOGENEOUS BALLS.

THE FIRST RUBBER-CORED BALL (THE "HASKELL") WITH CORE OF RUBBER THREAD WOUND UNDER TENSION AND COVER OF GUTTA PERCHA. FIRST USED IN BRITAIN IN 1902.

BRITISH IMPROVEMENT ON THE HASKELL, WITH LARGER CORE AND SOLID CENTRE.

FURTHER IMPROVEMENT; CORE AGAIN LARGER AND THE COVER MUCH THINNER.

STILL LARGER CORE AND "EGGSHELL" COVER.

A NEW DEPARTURE. DIAMETER OF BALL REDUCED FROM $1\frac{11}{16}$ INCH TO $1\frac{5}{8}$, WEIGHT IN PROPORTION.

BALL OF NORMAL SIZE BUT MUCH HEAVIER THAN BEFORE. FIRST BALL TO SINK IN WATER.

THE 1911 BALL. SMALL SIZE ($1\frac{5}{8}$") AGAIN AND MUCH HEAVIER THAN BEFORE; SINKS IN WATER.

Sketches of new developments for balls and cover markings, taken from *Frys* magazine 1911-12

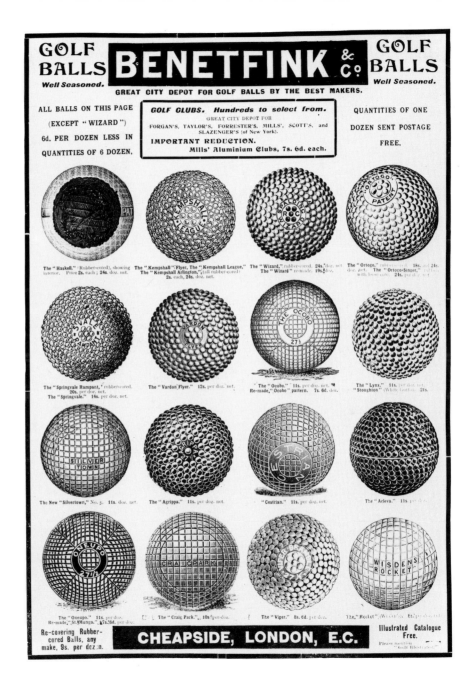
49

AVON
GOLF BALLS

IN THE JUNE COMPETITIONS
5 Cups, 15 Medal rounds,
9 "bogey" Competitions

were won with **AVON GOLF BALLS** during June.
Most of the winners have specially written in high
praise of their sterling qualities.

¶ And many new records for Courses were made,
particularly with the "Avon Junior" recessed—
the super-ball that good players love. This type is
the final answer to the problem of evolving a golf
ball that will drive long, low and true, run well
after alighting, and putt *obediently.*

"AVON RIFLED"
Standard Size, 27 dwts. (floating)
or 29 dwts. Junior, 30 dwts.

2/- each.

"AVON" Standard Floater,
Standard Heavy, or Junior
Heavy, each with Recessed or
Bramble Marking.

1/9 each.

your "Pro." or Sports Dealer does not stock, please write us. Trial Sample, post free, 2/- or 1/9.

At Prestwick Vardon, Simpson, Mitchell, and Williamson (finishing 1st, 3rd, 4th, and 5th), and many
others, were noticed with the handy **AVON BALL CLEANER** attached to their Club Bags.
This new Cleaner—"The Sponge in the Captive Cap"—is the cutest contrivance yet invented.
Price 1/- each.

Manufactured by THE AVON INDIA RUBBER CO., LTD., MELKSHAM, WILTS.
LONDON: 19 NEWMAN STREET, OXFORD STREET, W.
Depots also at BRISTOL, BIRMINGHAM, MANCHESTER, GLASGOW, and PARIS.

THE ZENITH 2/6

The Secret of the "Zenith" is in its wonderful core

—the core that looks like rubber—feels like rubber—is like rubber only, for its purpose is far, far better. It is made of a new and remarkable composition, the base of which is starch. It gives to the "Zenith" ball its "long-carry" and "short-run." It gives absolute reliability on the green—it gives comparative deadness of fall—it gives golf-ball satisfaction—satisfaction after the first game —satisfaction after each succeeding game.

The ZENITH PATENT CORE BALL

"**Golf Illustrated**" of **March 8th said**:—"Its great merit is in the comparative deadness of its fall both from full and approach shots. One can place the ball with it, feeling sure that it will not run after landing beyond all reasonable calculation. On the putting green its steadiness and reliability are equally remarkable."

Try the "Zenith"—you'll be as enthusiastic as other golfers are. Sample sent on receipt of 2/6. Sample of the "Bogey"— same core as "Zenith," only lighter—2/-. First ask if your professional or dealer stocks them.

R. LEHMANN & CO., LTD., Monument Street, LONDON, E.C.

NORFOLK STUDIO.

2/-

You can try the longest driving ball in the World

——FREE

To *prove* our faith in the quality and supremacy of Aero 'M' Balls, we hear and now offer to return your money in full, without delay or demur, if you buy one and are dissatisfied in the slightest particular. Ask your professional to supply you.

RECORDS MADE WITH AERO 'M'

May 18th.—A. S. Moses, Brecon Golf Club, created a new record for the course with a score of 73, using our Aero 'M' Golf Ball.

May 16th—S. Pearson, North Gloucester Golf Club, created a new record with a score of 71, using our Aero 'M' Golf Ball, the previous record being 73 by Abe Mitchell.

THE MIDLAND RUBBER CO., LTD., RYLAND STREET, BIRMINGHAM..

'AERO'
The Paramount BALL

54

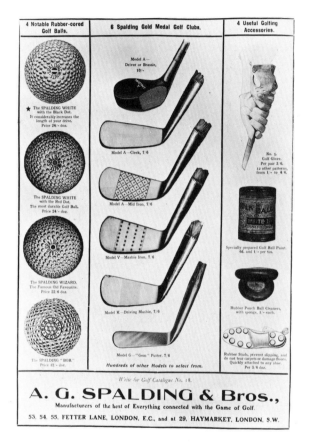

Early Clubmakers

Prior to the great golf craze which started in the last quarter of the nineteenth-century, the craft of making golf clubs and balls had been for many years confined to a few golfing families in Scotland where the art had been passed from father to son. These families were the Forgans, to whom the renowned H. Philp was related, the McEwans, the Dunns, the Patricks and the Parks. Here are staff photographs of R. Forgan & Son taken in 1881 and 1895

The McEwans

This club-making business was founded by James McEwan at Bruntsfield, Edinburgh, in 1770 and was carried on by three succeeding generations of the family until 1897

In 1847 they opened a branch at Musselburgh where at a later stage they also became ball-makers. This business was wound up in 1897

A group of old time professionals, Perth, 1864, including (1) Tom Morris, Jr. (2) Tom Morris, Sr. (3) G. D. Brown (4) D. Park (5) W. Dow (6) C. Hunter (7) W. Park (8) James Johnstone (9) J. Strath (10) R. Macdonald (11) R. Andrews

Peter McEwan 1834-1895

D. McEwan 1869-1921

Peter McEwan 1781-1836

MR. McEwan's Premises at Bruntsfield Links, Edinburgh.

Willie Dunn Sr., 1821-1871

Jamie Dunn 1821-1878

The Dunns

The Dunn Family story starts with the twin brothers Willie and Jamie of Musselburgh, the sons of a plasterer. Together they achieved fame as golfers in a number of celebrated challenge matches for wagers. In 1851 Willie was appointed 'Keeper of the Green' at Blackheath where he stayed for fourteen years and was joined by his brother Jamie in 1854

Willie had two sons Tom (1849-1902) and Willie Jr. (1865-1952). Tom became one of the early golf-course architects and laid out some 137 courses. Willie Jr. went to America, laid out the famous course at Shinnecock Bay, Long Island, and in 1894 won the first unofficial championship of the USA. He was also in demand as a golf-course architect

Willie Dunn, Jr., Champion of
America 1894

Tom Dunn 1849-1902

Willie Park Sr., 1834-1903

The Parks of Musselburgh

Old Willie won the championship in 1860, 1863, 1866 and 1875 and, having been apprenticed as a ball-maker, set up as a club- and ball-maker in 1870 at Musselburgh. His brother Mungo won the championship in 1874, and his eldest son Willie Jr. in 1887 and 1889 as well as taking part in many challenge matches. He published the first book by a professional golfer on how to play the game of golf in 1896 and *The Art of Putting*, probably one of the only books on that subject, in 1920

Willie Park Jr., 1864-1925 Champion Golfer 1887

The Park family made an outstanding contribution to golf in the hectic boom years at the beginning of this century. Willie Park Jr. was a dominant figure of those days, top class golfer, leading golf-course architect and maker of clubs

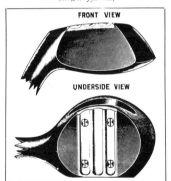

The Morris Family

Old Tom Morris was the son of a hand-loom weaver and is without doubt the greatest of all St Andrews' historical figures. He won the Championship Belt (precursor of the Open Championship) in 1861, 1862, 1864 and 1867 and his son Tom Morris Jr. won it outright by winning three times in succession 1868-1869-1870. Young Tom also won the first Open Championship in 1872 but died in 1875 following the tragic death of his young wife, much lamented as the finest golfer in his day

Old Tom became 'Keeper of the Green' at St Andrews in 1864 and in 1867 he set up his own club-making business which still survives today on its original site

'Young Tom' and 'Old Tom' Morris, *c.* 1873

Old Tom in later life

The Army & Navy Stores Catalogue *c.* 1900. Note that the public was still offered 'track-iron' style niblicks

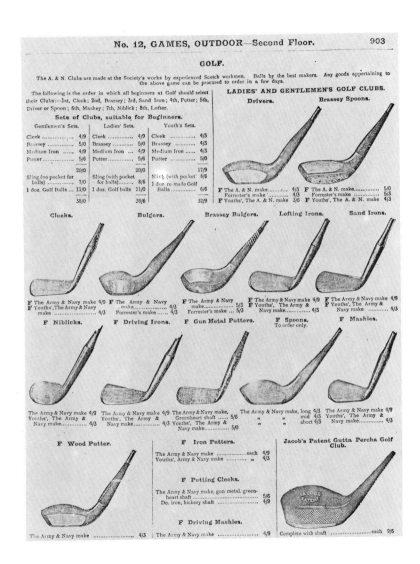

Advertisement (1910) by Charles Gibson of Westward Ho! Born in Musselburgh and apprenticed to the Dunns, he went to Westward Ho! in 1888

Ben Sayers in a bunker 1895 (The Redan Bunker, North Berwick)

Advertisement for Mills Aluminium clubs made by the Standard Golf Co., Sunderland. They produced clubs, mainly putters, from 1896 to the mid 1930s

‘Wee’ Ben Sayers and his son. Sayers (1857-1924) was a small man who originally trained as a circus acrobat; he often did cartwheels on the green when he holed a good putt

Slazenger and Sons catalogue — 1904

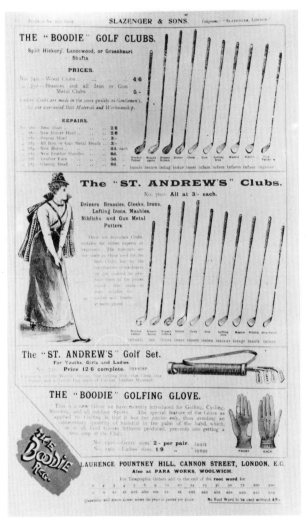

Wooden Clubs

Traditionally, the Keeper of the Green included in his duties the making and repairing of wooden clubs. He might be assisted by apprentices. The clubs were made or repaired by hand, and it was not until 1890-1900 that certain mechanical methods came to be employed. Clubs had individual characteristics, and owners, for this reason, preferred wherever possible to have them repaired rather than replaced. The relationship between the three parts of the club – grip, shaft and head – was complex and gave each club a unique feel which would have enabled its owner, even blindfolded, to identify it

The 'ancient' clubs of Royal Troon Golf Club. Features are the 'cut-off toe' shape of the irons; the shallow-faced, flat-lie woods. Several clubs have no grip.

On one of the clubs there is an emblem featuring a crown, a star and at the bottom a thistle with initials which could be I, J or T on the left-hand side and C on the right-hand side. A possible interpretation of this emblem could be, if initials are T.C., that it was made by Thomas Comb, clubmaker and owner of the Golf Tavern, Bruntsfield, Edinburgh in the mid-eighteenth century. He was succeeded as a clubmaker there by James McEwen who used a similar thistle mark on his club heads.

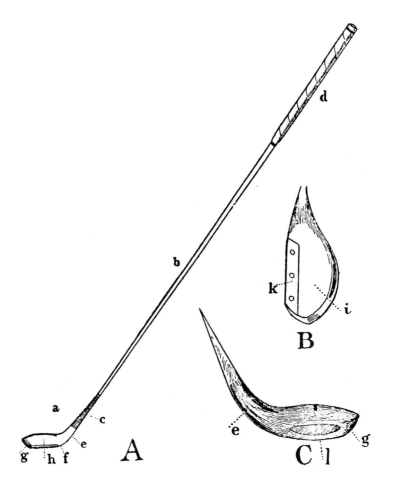

FIG. 1.—A WOODEN CLUB

A, the whole club; *B*, the 'sole'; *C*, back view of the head; *a*, the head; *b*, the shaft; *c*, the 'scare,' or part where head and shaft are fastened and bound together; *d*, the leather grip or handle; *e*, the neck; *f*, the heel; *g*, the toe or nose; *h*, the face; *i*, the sole; *k*, the bone; *l*, the lead.

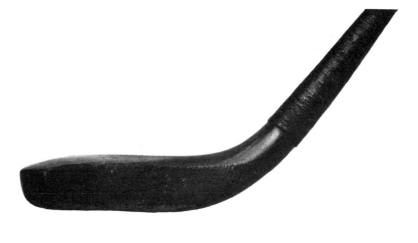

Two 'long-nosed' wooden club-heads
made in the nineteenth-century. The
shape of the head of the right-hand
club is typical of the first part of the
century, and that of the left-hand club
of the second part

A driver by Hugh Philip of
St Andrews

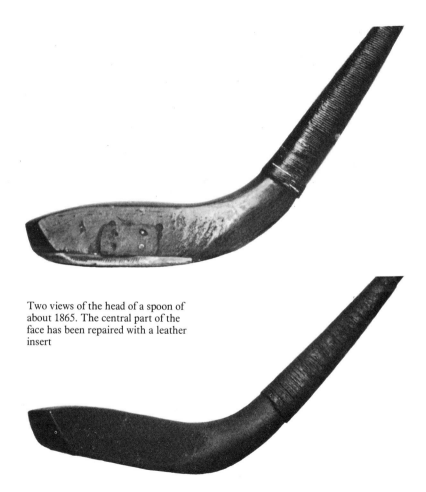

Two views of the head of a spoon of about 1865. The central part of the face has been repaired with a leather insert

The head of a baffing spoon. This club, shallow-faced and well-lofted, was used for approach shots before the days of iron play

A brassie by Harry Vardon, probably 1900. The small head is typical of this era, as is the exceptionally long, fine splice or scare. This club has a brass sole, hence its name. Beneath the brass is a horn insert in the leading edge. Forerunner of the number 2 wood

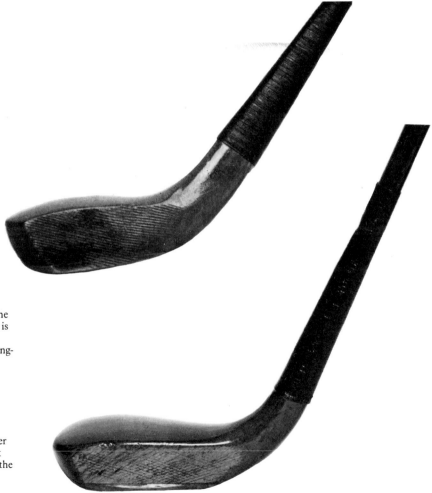
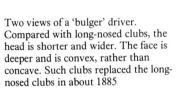

Two views of a 'bulger' driver. Compared with long-nosed clubs, the head is shorter and wider. The face is deeper and is convex, rather than concave. Such clubs replaced the long-nosed clubs in about 1885

A putter by H. Philp. Hugh Philp (1782-1856) was Master Club-maker of St Andrews. His nephew, Robert Forgan (1824-1900), joined him in the business and took over when Philp died.

The great amateur, George Glennie, putting at Blackheath with a putting cleek, c. 1885. It will be seen that the green is merely an extension of the fairway. There is no bag for carrying clubs. The players all wear jackets

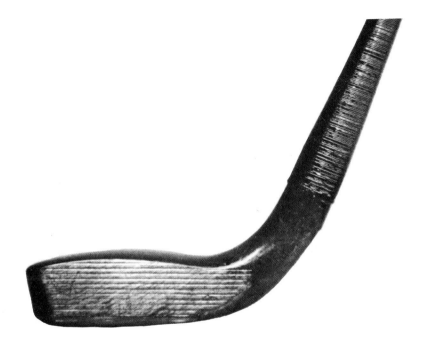

A wooden putter, made by William Park Jr., c. 1885

A scared-head club; somewhat more upright in lie than the other woods and with little loft. The shaft would be bowed, i.e. curved in the axis of toe to heel

The Iron Clubmakers and Iron Clubs

J^N GRAY

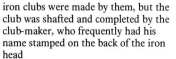

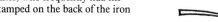

Line drawings of cleek marks of various cleek-makers, the general term for iron club-makers. The heads of iron clubs were made by them, but the club was shafted and completed by the club-maker, who frequently had his name stamped on the back of the iron head

Photos of cleek marks on clubs

In this picture, above the pipe of Stewart, the cleek-maker, is stamped the name of the man who shafted it, completed it and sold it

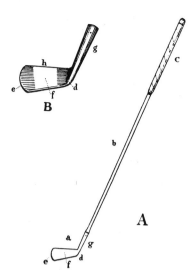

A. Wooden shafted iron club
B. Iron head with smooth face

A Philp/Forgan putter. This club has, in addition to a scared or scarffed joint, a long, narrow tongue-like mortice joint

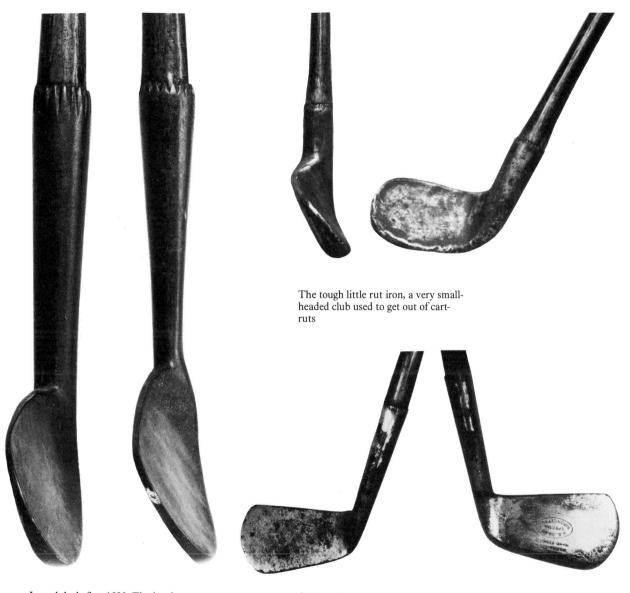

The tough little rut iron, a very small-headed club used to get out of cart-ruts

Iron clubs before 1830. The heads were blacksmith-made and the hammer marks can be seen in the faces, which are 'dished'

A 'tinned' mashie — a method of preventing rust

Two views of a lofting iron; precursor of the mashie, which in turn became a modern number 5 iron. 1875

Two views of a cleek, the earliest straight-faced iron. With modifications it became the modern number 1 and number 2 irons

Two views of a 'Maxwell' cleek. Holes were drilled in the hosel to lighten it

Two views of the mashie which first appeared in 1881 as a successor to the lofting iron

Two views of the 'Fairlie' niblick. This club had a hose, but no socket, thus eliminating 'shanking'

A putting cleek — a long, shallow face, like a cleek; it has less loft than a cleek, but more loft than a wooden putter. Useful, because of its loft, on rough greens

A wry-necked putter made by William Park, *c.* 1910. Park invented this shape of putter which is still in use today. It has less loft than the putting cleek

A 'water mashie'. The slots in the face allowed water (or sand) to pass through it

A selection of irons on the water mashie principle, offered for sale in a catalogue. The four clubs at the bottom, left and right, were known as 'rake' niblicks

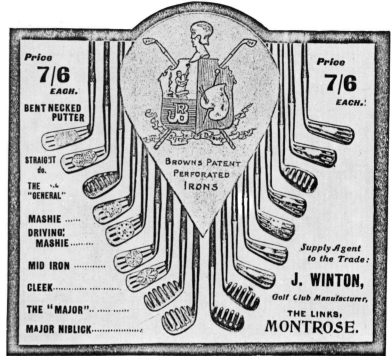

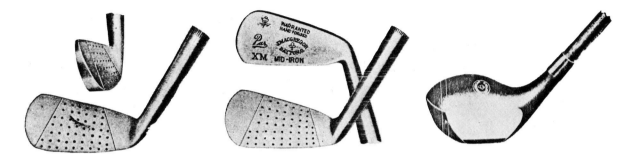

Guaranteed hand-forged par irons
from the catalogue of Crawford,
McGregor, Canby and Co. of the
USA. This firm was one of the first
American manufacturers of golf clubs,
starting in 1896

Golfing Styles

Tom Morris, showing the swing used for a feathery ball. Half way on the down swing. Note the flat plane in which the clubhead is swinging and the distance the ball is from the player. The stance is nearly square (but the ball being hit is a gutty, on this occasion)

The old palm grip. The club is held in the palm of the hands and not in the fingers. Common up to 1875

Two examples of the old St Andrews swing. Both elbows bent, the club dropped well down behind the back and almost touching the neck

Further golf swings. 2 and 3, the old St Andrews swing, showing the huge body turn. 1, 4, 5, 6 show less turn, the club near the horizontal and well clear of the neck: changes brought about by the improvement in golf balls towards the end of the nineteenth century

1

2

3

4

5

6

Various styles of putting

Harry Vardon and two aspects of his
swing. Note the bent left arm. 6, on
the previous page, is an earlier picture
of him

Patents

MR. PUNCH'S PATENT CADDIE CAR

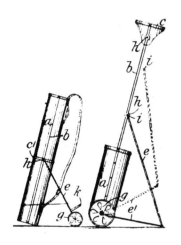

The golf trolley was first patented by Mr Boehmer in 1897. *Punch* produced an 'improved' version

Before 1890 there were only fourteen patents which had anything to do with golf. Thereafter there was a flood of ideas which the Americans added to within ten years, most of them aimed at making the game easier to play. At that time there were no regulations as to the size or weight of golf balls and no regulations whatever relating to clubs until 1908; golf balls came under control in 1922. Many ideas appear today which were first thought of at the turn of the century.

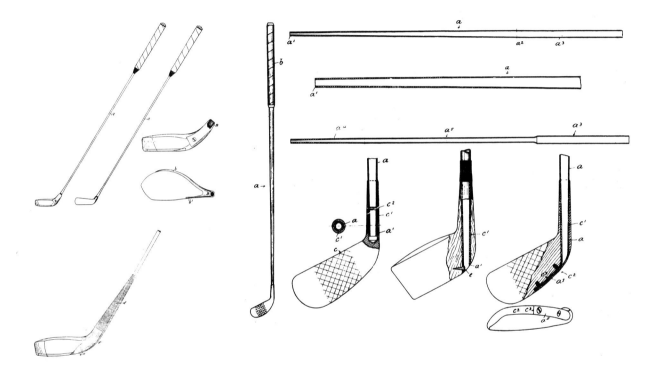

Steel Shafts

Mr T. A. Horsburgh of the Baberton
Club near Edinburgh in 1894 patented
and produced clubs with solid steel rod
shafts which were successfully used.
They failed to replace hickory-shafted
clubs because at that time the
professionals regarded them as a threat
to their livelihood

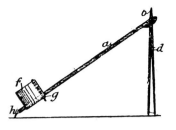

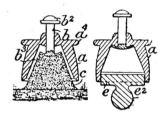

Above (top): a device for holding clubs and a tripod support, patented 1889; (centre) a device for moulding sand tees, and a rubber tee, both patented 1889; (bottom) mould for tees, patented 1885.
Below: ball pick-up, patented 1890

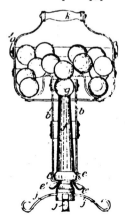

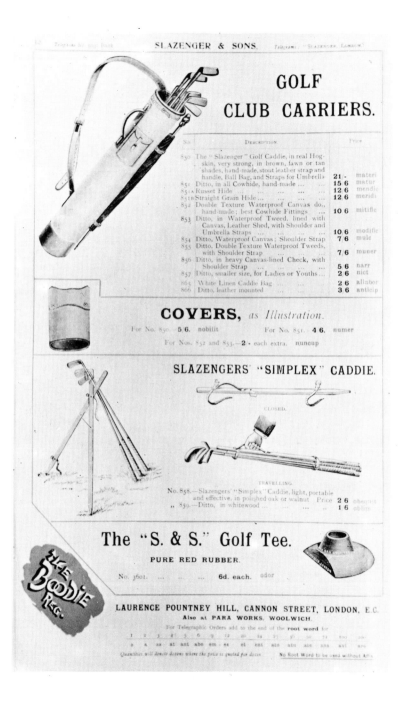

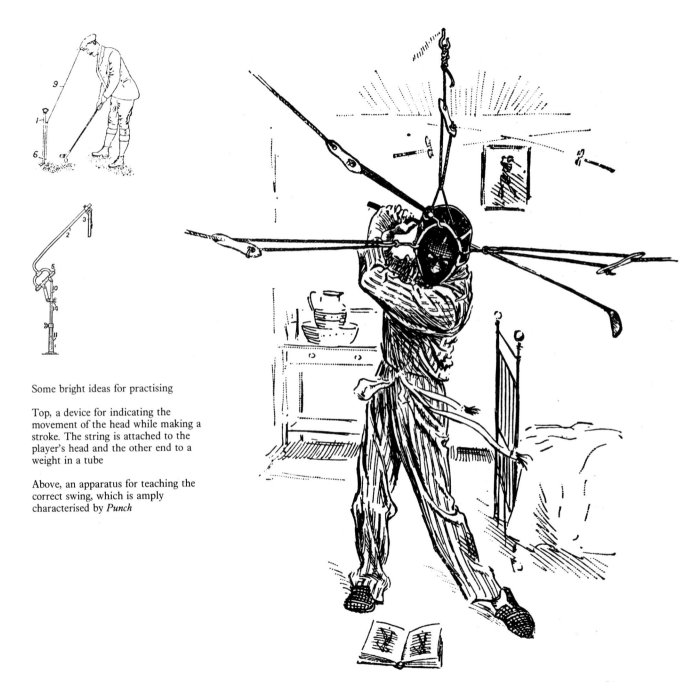

Some bright ideas for practising

Top, a device for indicating the movement of the head while making a stroke. The string is attached to the player's head and the other end to a weight in a tube

Above, an apparatus for teaching the correct swing, which is amply characterised by *Punch*

93

Golfing Costume

English golfing dress about 1875
There are no golf bags. The players
wear jackets and knickerbockers.
There are 'Tam O'Shanters' on some
heads — they were considered to lend
a Gaelic touch to the proceedings. The
caddies are barefoot, in contrast to the
slightly superior child in the lower
picture.

Advertisement for golfing attire 1875-1900

1 Jacket, tweed trousers and a bowler hat

2 The tweed knickerbocker suit

3 Similar; the caddie appears in some danger in this shot!

4 Knickerbocker suit

5 The 'Norfolk' jacket. Designed originally for shooting, it gave free shoulder movement

Advertisement for Ladies' golfing dress, 1875. Dress de rigueur — golf unlikely!

On windy days the long skirt could make it difficult to see the ball, so an elastic garter was worn at the waist, to be slipped down to about knee level to stop the skirt from billowing in the wind

1911. The lady manages very well despite the hat. She is showing an ankle!

1913. Miss Cecil Leitch wears a shorter skirt and spats over her shoes, and plays in a shirt and tie

W.J. Travis of the USA, winner of the British Amateur Championships, practising putting in 1904 with his centre-shafted 'Schenectady' putter. This type of putter was subsequently banned and remained so for many years except in the USA

1

2

3

4
A view of Lady Margaret Scott,
showing a small bustle to add to
her problems

1 & 2 The swing of Lady Margaret
Scott, who won the first three Ladies'
Championships in 1893, 1894 and
1895. Despite the long skirt, the well
nipped-in waist, leg o' mutton sleeves
and a saucy boater hat, she has
achieved a very long backswing

3 A later swing (1900) with the club
horizontal

A Grand Match at St Andrews, 1850.
Painted by Charles Lees, R.A. The
players are dressed in swallow-tail
coats and three of them wear top hats
— the usual 'everyday' dress of the
landed gentry. There are no golf bags,
the clubs being carried under the arm

The Artisans' Golf Club, Northam,
Devon, 1888. They wear the working
man's 'everyday' dress; cloth caps,
jackets and serge trousers. No ties.
Boots with hob nails ('Tackety Boots')
much in evidence. They had no golf
bags because they could not afford
them, and only had a few clubs

A typical young caddie of about 1875. He has no shoes or socks and his trousers are probably 'cut-down cast-offs' from his master. There were no golf bags, so clubs were carried on the shoulder or under the arm. Most of the clubs are woods

Memorabilia

31.—THE DUFFER.

37.—A LONG PUTT.

16.—AN ANXIOUS MOMENT.
"This for a Half."

2.—TOM MORRIS.
The G.O.M. of Golf.

29.—THE "MASHIE."

32.—LADY MARGARET SCOTT.
Lady Champion 1893-4-5.

Part of a set of Cope Bros. cigarette cards

Old golf buttons. These form an
attractive addition to golf
memorabilia. They are of many
metals: gold, silver-gilt, silver,
silver plate. Only members were
permitted to wear the Club button on
a blazer

Morrissian Ware vase — Height 8¾
inches Doulton

Pale green vase with tinted print by C. Dana Gibson (1867-1944) the American artist who immortalised the 'Gibson Girls' of English music-hall fame. The sketch is entitled 'Is a Caddie really necessary?' Made at Royal Doulton, England

Two dishes, with transfer prints of golfers. Made by Minton, England 1901

Punch bowl from Royal Blackheath Golf Club (nineteenth-century) and (below) enlargement of the escutcheon

Tea-caddy in Continental porcelain. The decoration consists of part of 'The Blackheath Golfer', a portrait of William Innes and his caddie by Lemuel Francis Abbott (1760-1803)

A painting of the Blackheath golfer William Innes (1721–95), without doubt the best-known golfing portrait of all time. Painted in 1778 by L. F. Abbott, it has hitherto popularly been believed to have been destroyed by a fire at the Blackheath Club c.1800, although we now know that there was no such fire.

William Innes' memorial plaque in St Andrew's Undershaft Church, St Mary Axe, London states that he died without issue. A recent examination of his will, however, discloses not only that he was fabulously rich and left £700,000 but also that he had one natural son and four daughters by Agnes Palmer, all well provided for by their father. Major-General Palmer (1807–92) was his grandson and served with distinction in India. In his *Indian Life Sketches* he recorded his possession of the Innes portrait and its destruction in the burning of his house at the siege of Lucknow during the Indian Mutiny on the night of 30 May 1857, only the family silver being saved.

Happily, an engraving dedicated to the Society of Golfers at Blackheath was made c.1790 from which all subsequent reproductions were effected.

Two of the many coloured cartoons to illustrate The Rules of Golf, which were commissioned by the makers of Perrier Water: prints of them were used for advertising purposes. Perrier is a French company; on some of these cartoons the Rules are in both French and English

Then A Soldier. Full Of Strange Oaths ...

Seeking The Bubble Reputation Even In The Bunker's Mouth.

TRESPASSERS
WILL BE
PROSECUTED

PENALTY
BALL
OUT OF BOUNDS
TWO STROKES

Then The Schoolboy With His Satchel And Shining Morning Face.

Two lithographs from a set entitled
'The Seven Ages of the Golfer'
produced by John Hassall (1868-1948).
A 'send-up' of Shakespeare

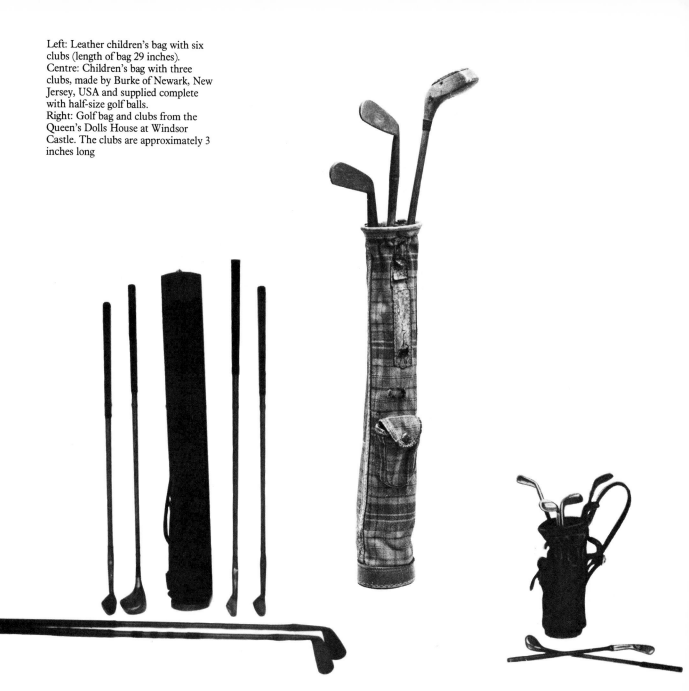

Left: Leather children's bag with six clubs (length of bag 29 inches).
Centre: Children's bag with three clubs, made by Burke of Newark, New Jersey, USA and supplied complete with half-size golf balls.
Right: Golf bag and clubs from the Queen's Dolls House at Windsor Castle. The clubs are approximately 3 inches long

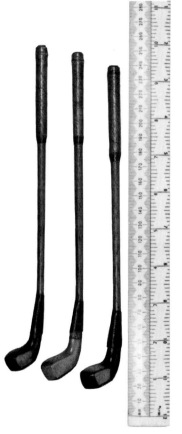

Left: The wooden clubs from the golf bag in The Queen's Dolls House supported by the hand of the maker, Charles Gibson of Westward Ho!
Right: Three miniature golf clubs made by W.H. Way, one of Charles Gibson's apprentices, who subsequently emigrated to the USA and, in later life, became President of the U.S.P.G.A.

William M. Goddard – a figure from
Charles Lees' 'The Golfers: A Grand
Match Played Over St Andrews Links'